ON TARGET WITH YOUR™ ASTHMA

TABLE OF CONTENTS

- **2** BREATHING BASICS
- **4** ASTHMA MYTH BUSTING
- **5** TYPES OF ASTHMA
- **8** TRIGGERS AND IRRITANTS
- **14** YOU'RE NOT ALONE
- **15** PREVENTING LUNG INFECTIONS
- **16** THE SMOKE-FREE SOLUTION
- **21** MEDICATIONS
- **27** PARTNERS IN CARE
- **28** USING YOUR INHALER
- **30** THE SPACER CONNECTION
- **32** THE MEDICAL POWER OF YOUR POWDER
- **36** REACHING YOUR PEAK
- **44** ASTHMA SELF-MANAGEMENT TREATMENT PLAN
- **48** CONTROLLING YOUR BREATHING
- **49** YOUR EMOTIONAL HEALTH
- **51** ASTHMA AND NUTRITION
- **52** MAKING MATTERS WORSE
- **53** ASTHMA IN SPECIAL GROUPS
- **55** ASTHMA IN PREGNANCY
- **56** ACKNOWLEDGEMENTS
- **57** FURTHER HELP

BREATHING BASICS

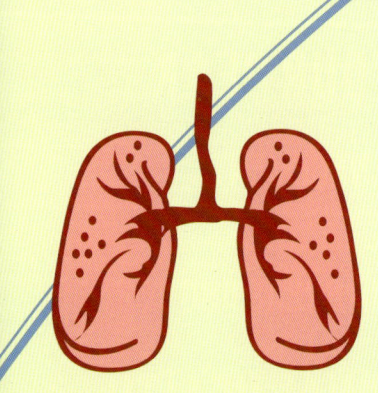

THE WORK OF BREATHING

HERE'S HOW THIS BREATHING THING WORKS: BREATHING BRINGS FRESH AIR INTO YOUR LUNGS AND REMOVES STALE AIR. THE FRESH AIR CARRIES OXYGEN TO YOUR BLOODSTREAM. YOUR HEART THEN PUMPS BLOOD WITH OXYGEN THROUGH YOUR BODY TO ALL YOUR ORGANS, WHICH NEED OXYGEN TO WORK SMOOTHLY.

FRESH AIR RUSHES DOWN THE THROAT AND INTO A LARGE AIRWAY OR BREATHING TUBE THAT BRANCHES MANY TIMES INTO SMALLER AND SMALLER TUBES. YOUR BREATHING TUBES ARE LINED WITH SPECIAL MUSCLES THAT RELAX AND CONTRACT WITH BREATHING. AT THE ENDS OF EACH OF THE SMALLER AIRWAYS IS A BALLOON-LIKE POUCH THAT EXPANDS AND COLLAPSES AS YOU BREATHE IN AND BREATHE OUT.

AS YOUR HEART PUMPS, BLOOD FLOWS THROUGH ARTERIES TO ALL YOUR ORGANS. AS THE BLOOD PASSES BY EACH ORGAN, IT GIVES UP SOME OF ITS OXYGEN TO FEED THE ORGAN, AND REMOVES THE WASTE GAS. WHEN YOU BREATHE OUT, THE STALE AIR IS PUSHED OUT.

SO WHAT IS ASTHMA?

So, that whole breathing thing sounds pretty plain and easy, right? Well, not for people with asthma. Asthma is a disease that affects the breathing tubes of the lungs. Those with asthma have sensitive breathing tubes that react to everyday things. These are called TRIGGERS. People with asthma have times when breathing is hard when they are exposed to triggers. These times are called asthma **attacks** or **episodes**.

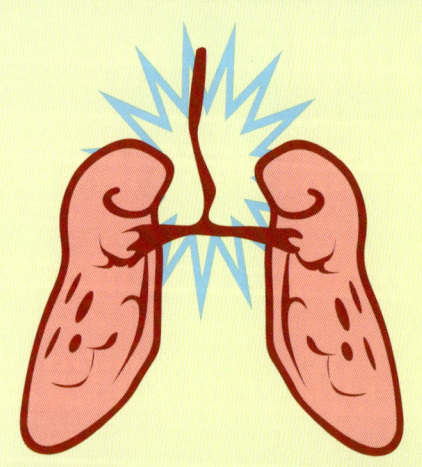

ATTACK!

WHAT HAPPENS DURING AN ASTHMA ATTACK?
- The breathing tubes in lungs become swollen (inflammation)
- The muscles that surround the airways start to tighten (bronchoconstriction)
- Extra mucus clogs the smaller breathing tubes

These changes slow the air that most often flows smoothly into and out of the lungs. Think about blowing air through a tube the size of a garden hose, then through a straw. The size of the tube makes a big difference in being able to push air through it. Breathing gets harder as you try to force air through the thin breathing tubes.

ASTHMA SYMPTOMS

- Wheezing or whistling sound while breathing
- Coughing and spitting up mucus
- Chest tightness
- Shortness of breath

Some people may describe an asthma episode as not being able to get enough air into their lungs. But, the changes that happen make the breathing tubes too small to let out the stale air.

AFTER AN ASTHMA EPISODE

You may feel that your symptoms have gone away and your breathing has returned to normal after an attack. But the breathing tubes are still swollen and sensitive. There's no cure for these sensitive breathing tubes. But there are things that you can do to care for your asthma.

WHAT ARE THE CAUSES OF ASTHMA?

We don't know. Sorry. But we do know about the risk factors that can cause asthma.

- **Allergies:** The American Lung Association says that at least 80% of children with allergies have asthma. For adults it's 50%.
- **Family History:** A strong family history of asthma has been linked with having the disease.

ASTHMA MYTH BUSTING

There are many things that people believe about asthma that just aren't true. It's good to set apart the truth from the myths when it comes to knowing about the disease. Keep in mind, knowledge is power. Use your brain and your knowledge as a weapon in the fight to be healthy.

MYTH	MYTH BUSTED!
You can get addicted to using inhalers.	Inhalers are not habit-forming or addictive. They are a good way to control your asthma every day.
You won't always have asthma. It comes and goes over time.	The symptoms may come and go, but if you have asthma, it's always there. Asthma is a chronic (long duration) disease that needs to be treated with medicine on a regular basis, even when no symptoms occur.
You can't play sports or exercise if you have asthma.	While exercising in cold, dry air can trigger an episode in some people, exercise is a good idea for everyone. Take your medicine and you can play sports, run and exercise. Swimming is good for asthma.
You can't lead a normal life if you have asthma.	*Please.* Even with asthma, you'll be able to lead as normal a life as you can. Follow what your doctor tells you, learn about your asthma, use your inhaler and stay away from your triggers. Don't let asthma get in the way of your life.
Asthma is contagious and can be caught from other people.	Wrong. Asthma isn't an infection and can't be spread from person to person.
You can outgrow asthma as you get older.	Asthma is a lifelong condition. A child's lungs can grow and handle it better, but asthma is forever.
Asthma can be cured.	Nope. While modern medicine keeps searching for treatment options, a cure for asthma has yet to be found. But managing asthma can be done with regular treatment.

TYPES OF ASTHMA

Asthma comes in many shapes, sizes and forms. These are the different types of asthma from which you may be suffering.

ALLERGIC ASTHMA

People with allergic asthma may suffer symptoms when they come in contact with an allergen, a common substance such as dust, animal dander, plant pollen and mold spores. Allergies happen when the person's immune system can't handle these substances. A special skin test may find out about your allergies.

Some common symptoms of allergies:
- Itchy, watery eyes
- Stuffy or runny nose
- Sneezing
- Headache
- Dark circles under eyes

ALLERGIC RHINITIS/HAY FEVER

Rhinitis attacks the inside of your nose, causing it to swell after you come in contact with an allergen. Symptoms are a runny nose, sneezing and congestion, sometimes mistaken for a cold. Like asthma, rhinitis may make your breathing tubes more swollen.

IMMUNOTHERAPY/ALLERGY SHOTS

If you have allergies, your doctor may suggest a shot to lessen your allergy symptoms. You may get allergy shots over many months or years, given weekly and then slowly reduced to once a month. This lets you slowly build up your immunity to the allergen. You may need allergy shots if:

- You have medium to strong allergy symptoms
- Your symptoms happen most of the year
- Your symptoms don't clear up with allergy medications
- You are sensitive to pollen, dust mites or other allergens that aren't easy to avoid

Allergy shots aren't for everyone with asthma and allergies. Talk to your doctor to find out if allergy shots will work for you.

SEASONAL ASTHMA

Allergens or weather changes can trigger seasonal asthma. A person with seasonal asthma may be allergic to pollen or mold around in different seasons. Others are sensitive to the cold air in the winter or the heat and humidity of summer. Unfortunately, there is no climate that is good or bad for all people with asthma. Cold winter days may be rough for people sensitive to cold air. But the wintertime may be better for someone with pollen allergies. Taking certain asthma medications at the start and throughout the season may keep you from getting seasonal asthma.

NON-ALLERGIC ASTHMA

People with non-allergic asthma don't have allergies but suffer the same symptoms. They can be sensitive to things like:
- Smoke
- Emotional stress
- Weather changes
- Respiratory infections

ASTHMA DUE TO EXERCISE

Asthma due to exercise may occur in people who have allergic and non-allergic asthma. The signs are triggered by changes in temperature and humidity that occur while being active. Because you tend to breathe through your mouth during exercise, cold dry air hurts the breathing tubes.

IMPORTANT!

DON'T LET ASTHMA KEEP YOU FROM EXERCISING!

It's important for all people with asthma to stay active.

Normal exercise helps to make stronger bones and muscles, and fight off infections. It makes your mental health and self-image better. Work closely with your doctor and follow a treatment and fitness plan to control your asthma.

PHYSICAL ACTIVITY TIPS FOR THOSE WITH ASTHMA DUE TO EXERCISE

- You may need to take asthma medications before doing activities.
- Don't be too active on days when your asthma isn't under control.
- Don't exercise outside on high pollen count days or during times of high pollution.
- Exercise at your own pace.
- Don't exercise in cold or hot weather.
- Warm up and cool down before and after exercise.
- Try other types of physical activities. Some people with asthma have less trouble swimming than running. Figure out what works for you.

NOCTURNAL ASTHMA
"SLEEPING ASTHMA"

A person with NOCTURNAL ASTHMA may have symptoms that get worse in the middle of the night.

Think of it this way: During the day, our bodies make hormones that act like soldiers, protecting us against asthma. But at night, these soldiers chill out, reaching their lowest levels and making us prone to attack.

THESE FACTORS MAY ALSO MAKE ASTHMA SYMPTOMS WORSE AT NIGHT

- Postnasal drip and sinus infections
- GERD: Gastro-esophageal reflux disease (acid from the stomach moving backwards into your esophagus)
- Allergens in the bedroom
- A late reaction to something that you were exposed to earlier
- Cool nighttime air

If you have more asthma symptoms at night than during the day, talk to your doctor. Your doctor may be able to figure out the cause and change your medications, giving you more nighttime troops to fight for you.

TRIGGERS AND IRRITANTS

A SENSITIVE SUBJECT

People with asthma have sensitive airways. Things that wouldn't usually cause breathing problems for most people may do so in a person with asthma. These troublesome things are called **triggers**.

There are two types of asthma triggers:

ALLERGEN — A substance that can trigger allergies. These things cause your breathing tubes to swell and extra mucus to build up.

IRRITANT — Not a substance that causes an allergic reaction, but something that can bother your breathing tubes and trigger asthma symptoms.

THE KEY TO SELF-MANAGING YOUR ASTHMA

Stop symptoms and control your asthma by staying away from allergens and irritants. That's the key. There's good news and bad news about these allergens and irritants, but these ideas for staying away from them can help! Making these changes won't cure your asthma but it may keep episodes from starting and help you breathe better. And that's always good.

OUTDOOR ALLERGENS

POLLEN AND MOLD

THE BAD NEWS
Pollen and mold are anywhere you find trees, grass and weeds. So unless you live in a plastic bubble it's going to be hard to keep away from these microscopic bothersome creatures.

THE GOOD NEWS
You may be able to lower your contact with pollen and mold by minding local allergen reports. Stay inside during pollen alerts, keep your windows and doors closed and run your air conditioner. You may not be able to beat them, but you can hide from them.

Before heading to other places on trips, find out what allergens are there. Stay away from wet leaves and fallen wood, standing water and places of bad drainage, which are sources of molds. Wear a mask for yard work, and shower and wash your hair after outdoor events.

INDOOR ALLERGENS

DUST AND DUST MITES

THE BAD NEWS
House dust has a lot of things like tiny pieces of fabric, particles of food, flakes of skin and protein from plants and animals. Dust mites survive on these items and humidity. A protein in their waste product triggers asthma and allergy symptoms. You can't completely get rid of dust mites from your home.

THE GOOD NEWS
There are solutions that can help lower their levels.

Use a wet mop and damp cloth when cleaning to keep your home dust-free.

Remove carpets. If that's not possible, clean them regularly. Have a friend vacuum with a HEPA filter so the dust doesn't bother you.

Get rid of drapes and mini-blinds on windows. Replace them with washable curtains or vinyl shades that don't trap dust.

Cover your pillows, mattress and box spring with allergen-proof encasements.

Wash bedding weekly in very hot water.

Remove clutter such as stuffed animals, knick-knacks, books and bookshelves.

Use a dehumidifier or air conditioner to keep the humidity level below 50% in your home.

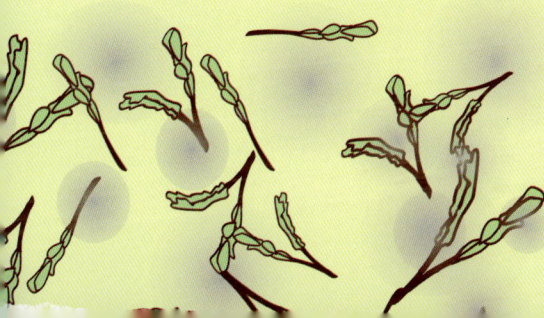

ANIMALS AND PETS

THE BAD NEWS

Some people may be allergic to an outdoor allergen that their pet brings in on its fur. In other cases, they are allergic to the protein found in animal dander, urine, and saliva. These proteins are very small and they can travel throughout your home in the air.

THE GOOD NEWS

Take these steps if you have pets that cause your asthma to become worse:

- Find a new home for your pet or keep the pet outdoors.
- Keep the animal out of your bedroom and other places where you spend a lot of time.
- Bathe your pet once a week.
- Vacuum your floors once a week with a HEPA filter.
- Remove carpets. If that's not possible, have them cleaned often.

COCKROACHES

THE BAD NEWS
Like dust mites, the protein in the waste of cockroaches can cause problems for asthma sufferers.

THE GOOD NEWS
Getting rid of cockroaches will help this problem. Cockroaches need three things to survive: water, food and humidity. Get rid of those things and you can get rid of the cockroaches.

- Seal places where cockroaches can enter your home.
- Fix leaky water faucets and pipes.
- Hire an exterminator to spray while you're away.
- Never leave food out.
- Wash dishes right away after eating.
- Vacuum and sweep floors.
- Take out garbage often.

INDOOR MOLDS AND MILDEW

THE BAD NEWS
Molds and mildew live in places of your home that are damp and humid. They send out small spores into the air and can trigger asthma.

THE GOOD NEWS
By limiting the moisture in your home you can control the mold.

- Use a dehumidifier to keep the indoor humidity level less than 50%.
- Clean bathtubs and sinks three to four times a week.
- Clean the drip pan under the refrigerator once a month.
- Clean the garbage can with mild detergent.
- Don't put in carpet on concrete.
- Remove indoor plants.
- Vent your clothes drier to the outside.
- Clean the inside and outside of your air conditioner.

FOODS

THE BAD NEWS
Food allergies are rare and mostly found in children, but even they can cause asthma attacks. The most common food allergens are cow's milk, eggs, peanuts, soybean products, shellfish, corn and wheat.

THE GOOD NEWS
By staying away from processed foods and those with allergens that harm you, you can keep from having asthma episodes. Make sure to read food labels, checking for ingredients that can harm you.

MEDICATIONS

THE BAD NEWS
Some over-the-counter medications such as aspirin and most often prescribed medications such as non-steroidal anti-inflammatory and beta-blockers may not improve your asthma symptoms.

THE GOOD NEWS
It's important to know your allergies and try to stay away from them. By making sure your doctors know that you have asthma, they can prescribe medications for you that don't make asthma conditions worse.

IRRITANTS

AIR POLLUTION

THE BAD NEWS
People with asthma are more sensitive to sources of indoor and outdoor air pollution. These are traffic, high ozone levels, smoke, gases, and fumes.

THE GOOD NEWS
You can fight these sources by taking these steps:
- Stay indoors when the air is smoggy or traffic is heavy with smoke and fumes.
- Stay away from places with heavy smoke, smog or power plants.
- Don't pump gas yourself, and keep your car windows closed during fueling to keep from breathing the fumes.
- If you have to use a fireplace or wood-burning stove, make sure it's well ventilated.
- Don't use kerosene heaters.
- Always use fans to remove any fumes or smoke while cooking.
- Don't let others smoke in your home.
- Reserve smoke-free hotel rooms and rental cars.

STRONG ODORS

THE BAD NEWS
Even odors from perfumes, after-shave, cologne and cleaning products can bother your breathing tubes and trigger an attack.

THE GOOD NEWS
Not using aerosol sprays, chemical products like ammonia, chlorine bleach and other products with strong odors can save you from an asthma episode. Use roll-on deodorants, liquid or gel personal hygiene products instead of aerosol sprays.

CHANGES IN THE WEATHER

THE BAD NEWS
Changes in the temperature and humidity, barometric pressure, or strong winds, may cause more symptoms for a person with asthma.

THE GOOD NEWS
Wearing a scarf or mask over your mouth and nose can help. When it's hot and humid, don't exercise or work outdoors.

INFLUENZA (FLU)

THE BAD NEWS

Watch out. It comes back each year. The flu is a virus that strikes quickly and spreads even faster. It's easy to mistake a common cold for the flu, but cold symptoms are milder and most often don't last as long.

Know these flu signs:

- Fever
- Muscle aches
- Feeling weak and tired
- Sore throat
- Cough

MORE BAD NEWS

When you have asthma and you get the flu, you're more likely to feel asthma symptoms and get lung infections.

THE GOOD NEWS

Not getting lung infections from the flu is your best course of action. Get a flu shot every year as soon as it's on hand, usually in the early fall. Some people worry that the shot will give them the flu, but that's not possible. The shot is made from a form of the virus that has been killed.

ACUTE BRONCHITIS

THE BAD NEWS

Viral or bacterial infections can attack asthma sufferers, causing a swelling in the lower breathing tubes and a productive cough. This is acute bronchitis. Look for these signs:

- A moist cough
- Clear or colored mucus
- Wheezing
- Shortness of breath

THE GOOD NEWS

Well, there isn't any, really. Most often acute bronchitis is caused by a viral infection and doesn't react to antibiotics, so you're forced to let the infection run its course and wait till the signs clear. Ugh.

PNEUMONIA

THE BAD NEWS

When you have asthma, you're also more likely to get pneumonia, especially during the winter months. Pneumonia may happen after you're exposed to a virus or bacteria. It causes your breathing tubes to swell and fill with mucus, making it harder to breathe. Signs for pneumonia:

- Fever
- Shortness of breath
- Change in amount or color of mucus

THE GOOD NEWS

Ask your doctor about a pneumonia shot. Most people only get the pneumonia shot once in their lifetime but you may need a booster after age 65 if you haven't had one in the last five years.

YOU'RE NOT ALONE
FAMOUS PEOPLE THROUGH HISTORY WHO SUFFERED FROM ASTHMA

POLITICIANS

Martin Van Buren
8th president of the U.S.
Theodore Roosevelt
26th president of the U.S.
Woodrow Wilson
28th president of the U.S.
Calvin Coolidge
30th president of the U.S.
John F. Kennedy
35th president of the U.S.
William Tecumseh Sherman
Civil War general
Peter the Great
Russian Czar
John Locke
Politician, philosopher
Walter Mondale
42nd vice president of the U.S.

ENTERTAINERS

Bob Hope
Actor, comedian, entertainer
Steve Allen
Comedian, actor
Robert Joffrey
Dancer, choreographer
Paul Sorvino
Actor
Martin Scorsese
Film director
Loni Anderson
Actress
Jason Alexander
Actor, director
Morgan Fairchild
Actress
Judy Collins
American folk singer and songwriter
Elizabeth Taylor
Actress
Alice Cooper
American rock singer

AUTHORS & WRITERS

Samuel Johnson
Poet, critic, essayist
Marcel Proust
French novelist
John Updike
Author
Louis "Studs" Terkel
Author, historian, broadcaster
Edith Wharton
Author
Ambrose Bierce
Journalist, author
Charles Dickens
English novelist
Dylan Thomas
Poet, playwright

ARTISTS & COMPOSERS

Leonard Bernstein
Conductor, composer
Antonio Vivaldi
Composer, conductor
Ludwig von Beethoven
Composer

ATHLETES

Jim "Catfish" Hunter
Hall of Fame baseball player
Tom Dolan
Olympic medalist for swimming
Greg Louganis
Olympic medalist for diving
Jackie Joyner-Kersee
Track and field Olympic medalist
Jim Ryun
Olympic medalist runner
Dennis Rodman
Basketball player
Dominique Wilkins
Basketball player
Art Monk
Football player
George Murray
Wheelchair athlete and Boston Marathon winner

PREVENTING LUNG INFECTIONS

RISK FACTOR

When you have asthma, you're more at risk for lung infections from a cold or the flu. What can you do to keep from getting these illnesses?
Try these tips:

- Get the flu shot each fall as soon as it's ready. If you're allergic to eggs, ask your doctor before getting this shot.
- Ask your doctor for a pneumonia shot. Keep in mind that the pneumonia shot is not a substitute for the flu shot, you need both! It's safe to get the pneumonia shot and flu shot at the same time.
- Urge everyone in your home to get the flu shot.
- Try to stay away from people who have a cold or flu.
- Stay out of crowds, mostly during the winter cold and flu seasons.
- Wash your hands often, and try not to touch your face. Most germs are spread by touching your hand to your mouth.
- Eat a good, balanced diet and exercise regularly.
- Get plenty of sleep.
- Don't smoke.
- Keep your lungs clear of mucus, which can trap germs.
- Keep your respiratory gear clean and sanitized.

INFECTION! SIGNS AND SYMPTOMS

Don't wait to get a doctor's help. The earlier you do so, the sooner you can get the care you need. Signs and symptoms may be different for each person, but include:

- Fever or chills
- Sore throat and painful neck glands
- Shortness of breath, coughing, wheezing or a tight feeling in the chest
- A change in mucus, such as an increase in the amount, odor or color
- Feeling more tired and run down than usual
- Stabbing chest pain when breathing

Watch your signs and symptoms and call your doctor right away if you have any concerns.

THE SMOKE-FREE SOLUTION!

THE BIG CHOKE

Smoking when you have asthma is a really bad idea. Being exposed to cigarette smoke or even secondhand smoke can make it harder to keep your asthma in check. The quick fix? If you're not a smoker, don't start. If you are a smoker, stop. Today. Now. Stopping will help you manage your asthma and lessen the risk of other health problems.

NO GOOD REASON TO SMOKE

If you smoke, think about these facts:

FACT 1 Cigarette smoke contains about 4,000 chemicals. Many of these are harmful and some cause cancer.

FACT 2 Smokers are twice as likely to have heart attacks as nonsmokers.

FACT 3 Smokers are ten times more likely to get cancer than those who don't smoke.

FACT 4 Cigarette smoke is harmful to EVERYONE who breathes it, even family members who don't smoke.

QUIT SMOKING, FEEL BETTER, LIVE LONGER

Your health will start to get better right away after you quit smoking.

AFTER 24 HOURS	Your chances of a heart attack go down.
2 WEEKS – 3 MONTHS	Your circulation gets better and your lung function rises by up to 30%.
1 – 9 MONTHS	Your lungs are able to fight infection better. Coughing, sinus congestion, fatigue and shortness of breath go down.
5 – 15 YEARS	Your chance of stroke is reduced to that of a nonsmoker.
10 YEARS	Your risk of dying from lung cancer is about half that of a smoker who doesn't quit.
15 YEARS	Your risk of heart disease is that of a nonsmoker.

STOPPING ISN'T EASY

If you've stopped smoking, **CONGRATULATIONS**! You've taken a big step in self-managing your asthma. If you haven't stopped yet, here are some tips to help you succeed when you try next time:

- Use the calendar as a tool to drive you. Set a special date to stop, like your birthday or a holiday, and stick to it.

- Change up your routine to stay away from the places you most often smoke.

- Write out the reasons for not smoking and put them up everywhere you can see them.

- Get rid of your cigarettes, ashtrays, lighters and matches.

- Empty and completely clean car ashtrays. Fill them with some change to keep from using them for ashes.

- Involve your friends and family. Tell them about your plans to stop and ask for their support.

- Get a friend who smokes to stop with you. Quitters enjoy more success with a partner.

- Join a stop-smoking support group. Find out if your health plan has a support group or other programs. Your doctor may have some ideas about local programs.

- Get in touch with your Respiratory Therapist for info and support.

MEDICATIONS TO HELP YOU QUIT

When pure willpower and the right attitude aren't enough to get you through the cravings for cigarettes, nicotine patches, nicotine gum, nasal spray, inhalers and pills can sometimes help lessen your craving. But always talk with your doctor before using these. Here are some things you should know before using medications to help you quit:

MEDICATIONS TO HELP YOU QUIT (CONTINUED)

- A nicotine patch is worn on the skin, most often on the arm, and puts small doses of nicotine into your bloodstream throughout the day.

- Nicotine gum releases nicotine as you chew it. Chew it for 30 minutes at a time and only when you feel the need to smoke a cigarette.

- Nicotine nasal spray gives you the fastest relief from nicotine cravings, but you need a doctor's prescription to get it.

- You breathe in the nicotine inhaler through your mouth. It gives you nicotine as quickly as gum, and should only be used when you feel the need to smoke.

- Your doctor can prescribe pills that don't contain nicotine but help get rid of the feelings of nicotine withdrawal.

- Never smoke cigarettes while using the patch, gum, spray, inhalers or pills. Too much nicotine can cause a heart attack. Always follow the directions on the package.

- Be sure to tell your doctor right away about any side effects.

- Don't forget: check with your health plan to figure out if the cost of the patch, gum, spray, inhaler or pills is covered.

STRONGER THAN THIS: NO MORE RELAPSES

- Check your list of reasons for quitting often.

- Stay away from people who smoke or from places where smoking is okay.

- Fight the urge to smoke by using healthy substitutes like chewing on a toothpick, fruit, vegetable sticks or sugarless gum.

- In place of smoking, stay busy with activities like gardening, woodworking, or drawing that keep both your hands and mind busy.

- Reward yourself for your success now and then with a special meal or movie. Rewards also remind you of the good parts of giving up smoking.

CREATE AN "I CAN DO IT!" PLAN

Make a personal action plan and write it down:

To help me stop smoking, I will use:

I will change my daily routine so things don't remind me of smoking by:

When I feel the urge to smoke, I will:

Who can I call, if I need help?
Doctor: _____

What will I do if I slip up?

Ask your doctor to answer these questions.

When I quit smoking, how should I expect to feel?

If I have withdrawal symptoms, how long will they last?

Where can I get more help, if I need it?

Add any others you might have in the spaces below:

MEDICATIONS

MEDICINE TO THE RESCUE

Medicine has come a long way in easing common asthma problems. Your doctor may prescribe medication to help you breathe easier and help other medical problems. Take them the right way and these medications may keep asthma symptoms from happening. **Preventing your symptoms from occurring is the key to self-managing your asthma.** Be sure to ask your doctor what side effects may happen with the medicine he prescribes for you.

MEDICATIONS LIST

MEDICATION	WHAT THEY DO	WHAT I TAKE
Bronchodilators	Relax and open the muscles around the airways. Two types of medications are used to relax airway muscles. **Short acting** Give you quick relief of symptoms and last 4 to 6 hours. **Long acting** Last 6 to 12 hours; not to be used for quick relief of symptoms.	
Corticosteroids	Reduce, reverse and in some cases stop irritation, swelling and mucus build-up in breathing tubes. Three forms of corticosteroids: **Oral** **Inhaled** **Nasal**	

MEDICATION	WHAT THEY DO	WHAT I TAKE
Non-Corticosteroids	Stop swelling and mucus build-up when coming in contact with something that bothers you. Two types of non-corticosteroid medications: **Anti-Inflammatories** **Anti-Leukotrienes**	
Anti-Histamines	Stop the symptoms of hay fever allergies (itching, sneezing, runny nose and watery eyes).	
Expectorants & Mucolytics	Loosen mucus so that it's easier to cough up.	
Cough Suppressants	Stop a steady, dry cough that doesn't bring up any mucus.	
Antibiotics	Fight infections.	
Water Pills (Diuretics)	Get rid of any extra body water or fluids—sometimes prescribed for people with heart problems such as congestive heart failure.	
Digitalis Drugs (Digoxin)	Make the heart beat stronger and more regularly—sometimes given to people with heart trouble.	
Potassium/Calcium Supplements	Replace vitamins and minerals needed for managing heart rate, blood pressure, and making bones strong. These minerals are often lost due to certain medications, such as water pills.	
Anti-Depressants and Anti-Anxiety	Help stop feelings of depression and anxiety.	
Anti-Reflux	Help to stop heartburn or acid reflux that won't go away, which may cause ulcers, stomach bleeding and more harmful asthma symptoms.	

MEDICATION CONCERNS

Q Will I become addicted to my asthma medication?

A Addiction to asthma medication hasn't been noted as a regular side effect.

Q If I take my asthma medication all the time, will it stop working?

A This is not too likely. Your doctor can help you manage your prescription use.

TIPS FOR USING MEDICATIONS THE RIGHT WAY

- Learn your asthma early warning signs/symptoms and take your quick-relief medications as soon as symptoms occur.

- If your doctor prescribes anti-inflammatory or corticosteroids, take these every day. These ease the swelling in your breathing tubes where bronchodilators do not.

- Watch your medication use. If you're using your quick relief medication more than two days a week (not including for exercise), your asthma may not be in control.

MANAGING YOUR MEDICINE

It should be clear, but medicine works best when you do what your doctor says. If you don't take your medicine the right way, it might not help you and could even harm you.

So follow these tips for managing your medicine:

- Read the label with care before taking any medicine.
- Take the right amount of each medicine at the right time.
- Take the medicine the way your doctor taught you.
- Don't skip doses or change the amount of the medicine you take each time. It could hurt you.
- If your medicine doesn't have a label, call your doctor and ask for directions. Remember to write them down.
- Take your medicine in a room that is well lit so you don't mix up medicine bottles.
- Check expiration dates on your medicines. Expired medicines can hurt you and should be thrown away.
- If you have any side effects, tell your doctor right away.
- Place your medicines in a pillbox. Pillboxes remind you to take your medicine at the right time each day and can be found at any drug store. Some even come with alarms that alert you when to take your pills.
- Never share medicines with someone else. Sharing medicine can be harmful.
- Some medicines should not be taken together. Be sure your doctors and pharmacists know which medicines you take so no bad reaction happens.

MANAGING YOUR MEDICINE...

Before your next appointment, write down a list of questions like these about your medications:

- What am I taking?
- Why am I taking this?
- How should I take it?
- How long will I have to take it?
- What are the possible side effects?
- What other drugs or foods may interact with this?
- What symptoms should prompt me to call you right away?
- Should I take it with food or on an empty stomach?
- Can I drink alcohol while taking this drug?
- Where should I store the medication?

If your doctor prescribes a new medication or same medication at a different dosage, make sure that you ask these questions:

- Should I keep taking all of my present medications?
- Should I keep taking all of my present medications at the same dosage and just as often?

Your Daily Medication Plan

Keep a list of daily medications you take, including over-the-counter ones. This list will help you take the right medication and dose at the right time. Remember to update your list as medications and dosages change.

DAILY MEDICATION CHART

DATE:

MEDICINE	DOSE (TABLETS/ TEASPOONS/ PUFFS)	BREAKFAST	LUNCH	DINNER	BEDTIME	AS NEEDED	COMMENTS

PARTNERS IN CARE

TAKE CHARGE

This is your life. It's your asthma and your job to handle it. Doctors admire people who take an active role in their own care. Nurses, doctors and therapists are all on your team, but taking charge of your own health starts with you.

Here are a few smart tips to help you take a more active role in self-managing your asthma.

- Keep all of your appointments. Put a note on your refrigerator or bathroom mirror to remind you. If you can't make it there on that day, call right away and reschedule.

- Make sure you know your asthma. If you don't grasp something your doctor says, speak up right away and ask him to make it clear.

- Be ready. Write down your questions before the visit.

- Be honest and tell your doctor about your symptoms, problems and concerns.

- Take notes when you are with your doctor or nurse. You might not recall the details of the visit later.

USING YOUR INHALER

Okay. So you've got an inhaler to help you breathe. It's important to know how to use it the right way to get the most out of it. For your inhaler to work at its best, use it with a spacer tool.

If you don't have a spacer for your inhaler, follow these steps:

STEP 1 **Shake the inhaler** before using, then remove the cap from the mouthpiece.

STEP 2 **Open your mouth wide**, and place the mouthpiece 1 or 2 inches from your mouth.

STEP 3 **Tilt your head back slightly**, keeping your mouth wide open.

STEP 4 **Take a slow deep breath through your mouth**, press down one time on the canister.

STEP 5 **Hold your breath** for 10 seconds if you can.

STEP 6 **Breathe out slowly** through pursed lips.

STEP 7 **Wait 2-3 minutes** before repeating the dose.

STEP 8 **Put the cap back on** the mouthpiece after your last puff of medicine.

STEP 9 **Rinse your mouth** with water so your throat and mouth won't be bothered.

CARE INSTRUCTIONS FOR YOUR INHALER

Like any piece of useful equipment, taking care of your inhaler will make it last longer and perform better. NEVER store inhalers in a place that may have extreme temperatures, like in the glove compartment of a car or in a refrigerator. Clean your inhaler at least every three or four days or sooner if it seems blocked (releasing little or no medication).

TO CLEAN YOUR INHALER:

- Remove the metal canister from the plastic dispenser.
- Run WARM water through the plastic dispenser.
- Shake water from the dispenser and let air dry.
- Place the cap back on the mouthpiece.

In some cases, you may need to use your inhaler before it's all the way dry. If so:

- Shake off the extra water.
- Replace the canister.
- Test spray it in the air.
- Take your normal dose.

PLAN AHEAD

It's of great value to know how much medicine you have and how long it should last. Plan ahead for traveling, holidays, weather conditions and busy lifestyles. Make sure you have a good supply at all times. Remember:

- Going without your asthma medicines, even for a day or two, can cause you to have trouble breathing. Always have plenty on hand.

- The number of puffs available in a canister varies with the medicine. For each prescription, ask your pharmacist how many puffs are in your canister and keep track of what you use.

Check Your Inhaler

You can figure out the amount of medicine left in your inhaler by using this method:

Figure out how many inhaler puffs of a medication you need for a month.

For example, if you take two puffs, four times a day for 30 days, you'll use 240 puffs each month. If you know how many puffs are in your inhaler, you can figure the number of puffs left at any time during the month. Remember, if you take extra puffs you'll need to subtract the puffs from what is left in your canister. Keep a slip of paper with your canister to keep track.

THE SPACER CONNECTION

WHAT'S A SPACER?

A spacer is a small tube used with a metered dose inhaler that can help the medicine go deeper into your lungs, cause less mouth pain and make the inhaler simpler to use. You should use a spacer when you can, but not with a dry powder inhaler or breath-activated inhaler. To get the best results, use the spacer in the right way.

Spacer Instructions (With and Without a Mask)

- Remove the protective cap from the inhaler and spacer.
- Check inside the spacer for dust or other objects before each use.
- Place the inhaler mouthpiece into the end of the spacer.
- Hold the spacer and inhaler firmly, and shake four or five times.
- Breathe out as normal.
- Place the mouthpiece of the spacer in your mouth between your front teeth and seal your lips around the mouthpiece, keeping your tongue flat and under the mouthpiece. (If you use a mask, place the mask gently over the mouth and nose.)
- Push down on the end of the inhaler, and breathe in slowly.
- When you have taken in as much air as you can, hold your breath for five-10 seconds. (If you use a mask, keep the mask sealed on your face and breathe in and out five to six times.) If the spacer makes a whistling sound, slow down.
- Breathe out slowly through pursed lips.
- Rinse your mouth out after using the inhaler.

Remember to:

- Always use medicine the way you are told.
- Use only one puff at a time, and wait two to three minutes between puffs.
- Breathe in slowly to fill your lungs.
- After using, remove the inhaler from the spacer and replace the caps on both.
- Return the spacer to its plastic storage bag.

KEEP IT CLEAN!

SPACER CLEANING INSTRUCTIONS
(With and Without a Mask)

- Clean at least once each week or more often if you're having breathing trouble.
- Remove inhaler from spacer.
- Undo the parts that can be removed. (If you use a mask, gently remove mask from mouthpiece.)
- Soak the spacer parts in warm water with a mild detergent for 20 minutes.
- Rinse with clean, warm water.
- **Never** boil or put the spacer in the dishwasher.
- Shake spacer parts and set them on a clean area to air dry.
- Let the spacer parts air dry all the way before putting them back together.
- When dry, store spacer in a clean plastic bag.

THE MEDICAL POWER OF YOUR POWDER

DRY POWDER INHALER (DPI)

Dry Powder Inhaler is a form of inhaled medication, different from your MDI (Metered Dose Inhaler), but designed in the same way to get medication into the lungs.

DPI INSTRUCTIONS

- **Load your DPI** as the instructions suggest.
- Turn your head to the side and breathe out as usual.
- **Wrap your lips tightly** around the mouthpiece of the DPI.
- **Take a breath in very quickly** and deeply.
- If you can, **hold your breath** for 10 seconds.
- **Breathe out slowly** through pursed lips.
- **Wait two to three minutes** before repeating the dose.
- **Rinse your mouth** with water so your throat and mouth don't get bothered.

CARE INSTRUCTIONS FOR DPI

- Clean the mouthpiece of the DPI with a clean dry soft cloth.
- Keep your DPI dry. **Never** put it in water.
- Don't store in places where it gets very humid, such as in a bathroom medicine cabinet or above a kitchen stove.

NEBULIZER USE INSTRUCTIONS:

Nebulizers use oxygen, compressed air or ultrasonic power to break up medical solutions into small aerosol droplets that can be directly breathed in. It's therapy that works well on asthma. Always take your nebulizer treatment either before eating or one hour after eating. Never take on a full stomach.

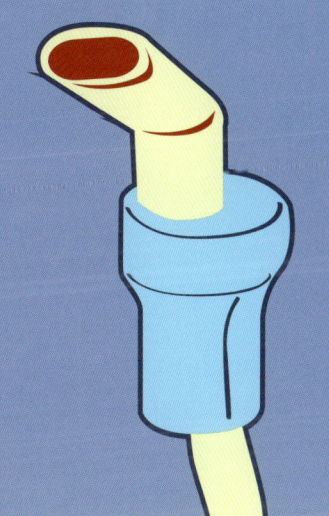

HOW TO USE THE NEBULIZER

- ◆ Wash your hands before you measure and get your medicine ready.

- ◆ Measure the medicine and put it in the nebulizer cup. Don't touch the inside of the cup.

- ◆ Attach the top to the nebulizer cup and join the tubing to the nebulizer and the compressor.

- ◆ Turn on the compressor. A fine mist will flow out through the mouthpiece.

- ◆ Place the mouthpiece securely in your mouth between your teeth and close your lips around it to make an airtight seal.

- ◆ Breathe in through the mouthpiece like you usually would, then hold your breath for one to two seconds. Remove the mouthpiece and breathe out slowly through pursed lips. The medicine will go deep into your lungs.

HOW TO USE THE NEBULIZER, CONTINUED:

◆ Tap the side of the nebulizer cup every two to three minutes.

◆ Keep taking the treatment until the nebulizer cup is empty. This may take 15 to 25 minutes.

◆ When you've finished, turn the compressor off and place a cover over the machine.

◆ Cough to bring up any mucus.

KEEP IT CLEAN! NEBULIZER CLEANING INSTRUCTIONS

Cleaning gets rid of germs, stops infection and helps your nebulizer last longer. Keeping your nebulizer gear clean is easy.

After each use:
- Rinse the mask or mouthpiece and T-shaped part in warm running water for 30 seconds.
- Let air-dry on a clean area.
- When fully dry, store in a clean plastic bag.
- **Once each day:**
  - Wash the mask or mouthpiece and T-shaped part with a mild dishwashing soap and warm water and let dry.
  - Put back in its plastic bag.

- **Never** put the nebulizer in the dishwasher.

Once each week:  REMEMBER

- After washing and rinsing the mask or mouthpiece and T-shaped part, soak them for 30 minutes in a mixture of one part distilled white vinegar and two parts water.

- Rinse under a strong stream of water for 30 seconds.

- Let air-dry on a clean area.

- When fully dry, store in a clean plastic bag.

Once a month:

- If you've been using your nebulizer each day, throw away the old nebulizer kit and tubing. Call your homecare supply business for a new kit and start using it.

SAFETY FIRST: COMPRESSOR SAFETY

Follow these rules below to use your compressor safely.

- Keep your compressor clean and dry.

- **Never** try to clean your compressor by placing it in water.

- Call your medical equipment business to tell them about any problems.

- **Never** try to fix a compressor that is broken or not working.

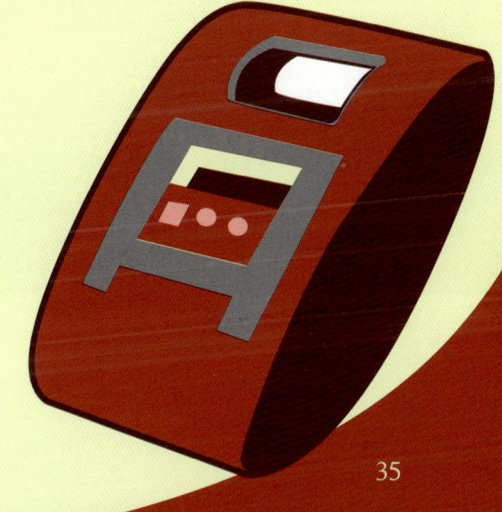

REACHING YOUR PEAK

Peak Flow Meter: What It Is, What It Does

A peak flow meter is a tool that measures how fast and hard you can blow air out of your lungs. When mucus, swelling and tightening make your breathing tubes thin, the air leaves your lungs slower. A peak flow meter is like a thermometer for your lungs, but it tracks breathing problems instead of temperatures.

GO WITH THE FLOW

Peak flow monitoring can help you...

- Track the triggers that make your asthma worse.
- Decide if you need emergency care.
- Decide if your lungs are tight before you have symptoms.
- Figure out if your treatment plan is working.

PEAK FLOW METER INSTRUCTIONS

1. Move the indicator to the base of the peak flow meter.
2. Hold the peak flow meter at the end away from the mouthpiece.
3. Always stand up.
4. Fully fill your lungs with a deep breath.
5. Put the mouthpiece of the peak flow meter in your mouth, between your teeth, over your tongue, and close your lips tightly around it.
6. With as much force as you have, blow out as quickly as you can. Pretend you're trying to blow out all the birthday candles at once.
7. Read the number at the level of the indicator.
8. Repeat these steps two more times.
9. Write down your highest number on the chart.

REMEMBER:
- Always give it your best effort or the reading won't be right.
- Write down your highest peak flow reading in the morning and again in the late afternoon.
- Write down your highest peak flow reading before and after using quick-relief medicine.

KEEP IT CLEAN! Peak Flow Meter Cleaning

Wash your peak flow meter once a week or more often if you're having asthma symptoms.

- Wash the peak flow meter in warm, mild soapy water.
- Rinse completely.
- Let it air dry before you measure again.
- NEVER try to clean the inside of the peak flow meter with a brush.
- NEVER boil or put the peak flow meter in a dishwasher.

"BEST" PEAK FLOW READINGS

Asthma is different for different people. You may have another type of asthma from someone you know who has it. Your symptoms, triggers and peak flow readings may be higher or lower than someone of your same age and height. So, it's important for you to find out your "Best" peak flow reading, that is, your highest peak flow reading.

How to Find Your "Best" Peak Flow Number

- Use your peak flow meter at least twice a day for two to four weeks when you're feeling well with no symptoms
- Record your highest readings in your Best Peak Flow Chart.

FORMULA FOR SUCCESS

Here's a useful formula to help you figure out your "Best" Peak Flow:

Take your three highest readings and add them together, then divide by three. For example, if you're three highest readings are 300, 310 and 320, when you add those three numbers together your base number is 930. Divide the 930 by three and your "Best" reading or average is 310.

300 + 310 + 320 = 930 / 3 = 310

A child's "Best" peak flow readings will change as he or she grows, so you may need to retake this reading every six months.

SYMPTOMS Check all that apply.						RECORD PEAK FLOW READING			
Wheezing	Coughing	Chest Tightness	Limited Activity	Night Awakenings	Early Morning Cough	Record your best peak flow each morning and early afternoon, before and a few minutes after using inhaler or nebulized medicine. AM	PM	Date	Triggers/PRN Medications* *Use as needed for increased symptions

KNOW YOUR ZONE

Once you've figured out your "Best" peak flow number, your doctor or respiratory therapist can figure your peak flow zones. These zones will help you to look for any changes in your peak flow readings. To make things simpler, the National Asthma Education and Prevention Program came up with a system in which the zones match up with the colors of a traffic light.

Your doctor may also give you lessons on what to do for changes in your peak flow readings.

GREEN ZONE
Your asthma is under control.

GO!

YELLOW ZONE
Your asthma is not under control and you should be very careful. Your doctor may give you instructions for your quick-relief medications and may even tell you to call his office.

CAUTION!

RED ZONE
ALERT!
Your doctor may tell you to call for medical care right away.

SEEK MEDICAL HELP!

EARLY WARNING SIGNS AND SYMPTOMS

Even though some people talk about their asthma episodes as asthma "attacks," they rarely happen without warning. Most people can tell when an asthma episode is coming. Think back to your last asthma episode. Did you have any early warning signs or symptoms? Early warning signs are those small changes that occur that may be connected with asthma that is getting worse. Symptoms are signs that clearly tell you it's an asthma episode. It's important that you notice early warning signs.

When these signs and symptoms show up, you can follow the instructions that your doctor gave you to care for your asthma. This may keep more serious problems from starting. Read over this list and check the signs and symptoms that pertain to you. Share them with your family, friends and doctor. Remember to change your list as others come up.

- LESSENING PEAK FLOW
- TIGHTNESS IN CHEST
- OUT OF BREATH QUICKLY
- TIRED
- SCRATCHY, OR SORE, THROAT
- STUFFED-UP, OR RUNNY, NOSE
- RESTLESS
- COUGHING
- BREATHING FASTER
- SHORTNESS OF BREATH
- ITCHY, WATERY EYES
- SNEEZING
- HEADACHE
- ITCHY BACK OF NECK
- HARD TO SPEAK
- COLOR CHANGE IN YOUR FACE
- WHEEZING
- OTHER (SIGNS THAT YOU IDENTIFY)

YOUR ASTHMA SYMPTOM SELF-ASSESSMENT CHART

Use this asthma self-assessment chart to track triggers, early warning signs, symptoms and medication needs. After looking at the information written in the chart, your doctor may make changes in your medication or asthma plan.

Use the charts in this booklet, or make your own. Your chart should remind you to write down:
- Date
- Symptoms
- Use of quick-relief medications
- Triggers that cause asthma symptoms
- Activity limits because of asthma

Wheezing	Coughing	Chest Tightness	Limited Activity	Night Awakenings	Early Morning Cough	Itching	Headache	Time of event AM	Time of event PM	Date	Triggers/ Quick-relief Medications

Comments: _____

Instructions for Increased Symptoms: _____

YOUR ASTHMA SYMPTOM SELF-ASSESSMENT CHART

Wheezing	Coughing	Chest Tightness	Limited Activity	Night Awakenings	Early Morning Cough	Itching	Headache	Time of event AM PM	Date	Triggers/ Quick-relief Medications

Comments: _____

_____

_____

_____

Instructions for Increased Symptoms: _____

_____

_____

_____

NOTES FOR MY DOCTOR

ASTHMA SELF-MANAGEMENT TREATMENT PLAN

STEP-BY-STEP INSTRUCTIONS FOR MANAGING YOUR SYMPTOMS

Your doctor may give you an asthma self-management treatment plan that is based on your history of asthma symptoms and present findings. The treatment plan gives you step-by-step instructions on how to manage your symptoms on a daily basis, as well as when you feel increased symptoms. Because the medication doses and how often you take them may differ at times, be sure you know these instructions.

WHEN TO SEEK HELP

Call your doctor if:

- Your peak flow doesn't improve after you've taken your quick-relief medications.

- Your symptoms don't clear up after taking your quick-relief medications.

- There's a change in your phlegm, such as the color, amount, or odor.

- You have a hard time breathing while lying down.

- You notice that you're more tired than normal.

- You notice swelling in your ankles.

REMEMBER

Quick-relief medications don't treat swollen, inflamed airways. Medications that ease swelling won't stop an attack of wheezing, coughing or choking. Used together, these medications can make up a treatment plan that works. Used one by one, they have very important but different roles. Treatment plans are matched to each person's needs. The goal is to keep the daily use of the quick-relief medication to a smallest amount by using other measures, such as staying away from asthma triggers and sometimes using anti-inflammatory medications.

NOTES FOR MY DOCTOR

Asthma Peak Flow Meter ActionPath™

GREEN ZONE

INSTRUCTIONS
(If your peak flow is _____ or higher)

Take these medications daily for your asthma

1. _____
2. _____
3. _____
4. _____
5. _____
6. _____

If you are having symptoms and your peak flow is ____ or higher, take _____
_____

Call your doctor if _____
_____

Take these medications before exercise: _____
_____
_____

If you are having symptoms or your peak flow reading is below _____ call your doctor.

YELLOW ZONE

INSTRUCTIONS
(If your peak flow is between ____ and ____)

1. Keep taking your Green Zone medications.

2. Take these: _____
_____
_____

3. Check your peak flow readings. If your peak flow is ____ or higher, call your doctor for follow-up instructions TODAY and keep taking _____
_____
_____

If your peak flow is less than _____, call your doctor NOW and keep taking _____
_____
_____

Add these: _____
_____
_____
_____

RED ZONE

INSTRUCTIONS
(If your peak flow is less than _____)

1. Take these RIGHT AWAY
_____
_____

2. Check you peak flow readings. If your peak flow is _____ or higher, call your doctor NOW Add these: _____
_____

If your peak flow is less than _____ repeat _____

Add these: _____
_____
_____

and call 911.

Name: _____
Date: _____
Height: _____
Weight: _____
Doctor's Name: _____
_____
Doctor's Phone Number: _____
_____
Emergency Phone Number: _____

Asthma ActionPath™ for Increased Symptoms

Name: _____

Date: _____

Height: _____ **Weight:** _____ **Age:** _____

Doctor: _____ **Phone:** _____

Daily Medications:
_____
_____
_____

Action for Increased Symptoms:
_____
_____
_____

Additional Instructions:
_____
_____
_____

CONTROLLING YOUR BREATHING

WHAT SHOULD YOU DO?

It's scary to have asthma and feel like you're winded and can't catch your breath. If this has happened to you, you know that gasping for air and breathing faster doesn't help. What should you do? Try these techniques:

PURSED-LIP BREATHING

Pursed-lip breathing helps breathing tubes stay open while you breathe out, letting you push out stale air that is trapped in the lungs. It may also help slow you down if you're breathing too quickly.

- Relax your neck and shoulders and breathe in slowly through your nose. Keep your mouth closed. (If you can't breathe through your nose, breathe gently through your mouth.)

- Purse or pucker your lips like you were going to blow out a single birthday candle.

- Breathe out slowly and gently through your pursed lips. Breathe out two to three times longer than when you breathed in. You may hear a soft whistling sound. Make sure you don't blow out your imaginary candle. If you think you have, you're still breathing too hard! With practice, this technique can become easy. You can use it any time you feel short of breath, even during physical activity.

YOUR EMOTIONAL HEALTH: IT'S THERE FOR A REASON.

Keeping Peace of Mind

Living with asthma and changing your lifestyle can make you feel upset, angry and unhappy. Here's a list of some actions you can take to make yourself feel better.

GAIN CONTROL OVER YOUR FEELINGS

You are not defined by your feelings. Anxiety, depression, and anger are normal. They happen. Accept these feelings, and try to work through them. Try writing in a journal, talking with a friend or family member, and joining a support group. You may gain more power over your feelings, once you learn to accept how you feel about having asthma.

THINK POSITIVE

It's hard to stay upbeat when you focus on the negative. You have the power to change! Having a good outlook on life can make your health better. Stay positive with these tips:

- **Let laughter be your best medicine.** Lighten up and share your laughter with the world.
- **Enjoy the small things.** There's joy all around us. Find it. Take time each day to think about the things that bring you joy.
- **Set goals.** Use your imagination and be creative with your goals. You could grow an indoor herb garden, learn a language or how to play an instrument – the possibilities are endless. Be true to yourself and try your best to meet each goal.

YOUR EMOTIONAL HEALTH: IT'S THERE FOR A REASON... CONTINUED

TALK TO OTHERS

It's important to talk to others. Your family, friends, teachers or people you work with can give you support if they know the facts. Choose the right time to tell each person about your asthma. The best time is at the start of a new school year, new job, in private, when you're not having breathing problems.

DEAL WITH ANXIETY AND PANIC DISORDERS

Anxiety and panic disorders are episodes of great fear. People who have anxiety or panic attacks often have strong chest pain, rapid heartbeat, shortness of breath, dizziness and pain in the abdomen. If you're having these symptoms, tell them to your doctor. The feelings of anxiety and panic disorders can be life threatening. Your doctor will need to see you in person to find the cause of the attacks.

STAY IN CONTROL

The bad news: It's impossible to stay away from all the situations that may trigger an anxiety attack. But you can come up with a plan that will help you deal with it. Take control of your attacks:

- If you feel a panic attack coming on, stop what you're doing and get in a comfortable position.
- Do some deep breathing exercises to control your breathing.
- Relax your muscles.
- Control your thoughts. Tell yourself that you won't die from a panic attack.

ASTHMA AND NUTRITION

EAT RIGHT, BREATHE RIGHT

Good nutrition has so many benefits, even for asthma sufferers. It helps the body keep from getting infection and lessens the symptoms of asthma and allergies.

- **A Healthy Diet** - A healthy diet contains fresh fruits, vegetables, nuts, seeds and whole grains. A diet rich in vitamin E may help lung function.
- **Food Labels** - If you have allergies and asthma, it's always good to read food labels. Know your triggers and stay away from them.
- **Know What You Need** - If you have a food allergy that cuts a whole food group from your diet, talk to your doctor about the vitamins or minerals you might need.

OMEGA-3 fatty acids may lower asthma symptoms by easing the swelling and pain in the breathing tubes.

Foods with Omega-3 Fatty Acids
Omega-3 Fatty Acids are found in oily fish such as salmon, tuna, mullet, and rainbow trout. Other sources are flaxseed, soybean oil, canola oil and dark green vegetables.

GET FLUIDS
The need for fluids is vital when dealing with asthma. You can ease asthma and respiratory allergy symptoms by thinning the mucus in the lungs. So what's the answer? Drinking plenty of water.

THE NEED FOR CALCIUM

Many people with asthma use corticosteroids to help them breathe comfortably. High doses over many years can raise your risk of getting osteoporosis. Osteoporosis is a bone disease that leads to bone loss and fractures. You can prevent this disease by taking calcium and adding more vitamin D in your food plan. Vitamin D helps the body to take in calcium.

- **Foods with Calcium** Foods rich in calcium are dairy products, tofu, raisins, sardines, and salmon with bones and dark green, leafy vegetables like broccoli, chard and collards.
- **Can You Get Enough Calcium?** Unfortunately, some people are either allergic to dairy products or can't digest them. As we get older we lose our ability to take in calcium. Sometimes other things we eat, such as large amounts of proteins and fiber, can also take away the body's calcium.
- **Calcium Supplements** Calcium supplements can help you to reach your recommended daily intake. Make sure you talk to your doctor because calcium supplements can block other medications and can cause abdominal side effects. Start with lower doses and work your way up.

MAKING MATTERS WORSE

"GERD IS THE WORD"

Gastro-esophageal Reflux Disease (GERD) may be to blame if you can't control your asthma symptoms or if they seem to get worse at night. GERD or reflux happens when a muscle in the stomach lets the stomach acid back up into the esophagus. This can make matters worse for your asthma.

If you're having any of these symptoms, talk with your doctor.
- Frequent heartburn
- Bitter or sour taste in mouth
- Hoarseness
- Cough that won't go away
- Chest pain
- A worsening of your asthma symptoms at night

If your doctor decides that you have GERD, he or she may choose a care plan for your asthma. This plan should greatly help your breathing.

Treatment options for GERD:
- Taking medications that help with acid
- Elevating the head of the bed six or more inches
- Not eating or drinking three to four hours before going to bed
- Staying away from certain foods (caffeine, chocolate, citrus, mint, carbonated drinks) and certain medications
- Not wearing tight garments
- Quitting smoking
- Not drinking alcohol drinks
- Losing weight

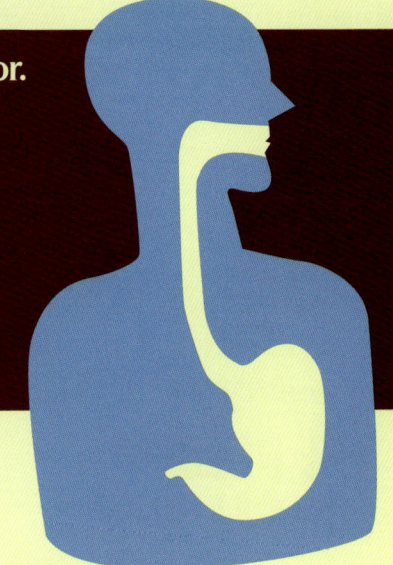

ASTHMA IN SPECIAL GROUPS

A NOTE TO PARENTS OF CHILDREN WITH ASTHMA

There are scary moments for the parents of kids with asthma. But with the right care, your child can live a normal life. You'll have added duties, concerns and tasks in order to keep your child safe and breathing freely.

If you have a child with asthma, keep these guidelines in mind:

- Make sure you work with your child's doctor to come up with a plan as soon as possible. This may include a list of daily medications and instructions for managing the symptoms.

- If your child spends most of his day in school or day care, make sure teachers and other caregivers know about your child's asthma and treatment plan.

- For older children, it's vital that they become involved in their own care. Talk to your child about his or her asthma and make clear what to do during an asthma episode. Review the treatment plan with your child so you both feel confident to handle symptoms when they occur.

- Make sure your child knows how important it is to carry his quick relief medication and use it when needed. Most children eight years old or older can do this.

- Keep a diary. Jot down everything you learn about your child's triggers and symptoms. Remember that these may change based on the season.

- Make sure your child takes his medication each day. Asthma is a condition that needs daily attention and doesn't just go away. Without treatment, asthma can cause serious changes in the breathing tubes. These changes may cause lasting harm to the lungs.

- If you smoke cigarettes, never smoke around your child. The smoke will make your child's asthma symptoms worse. It's another great reason to quit smoking for good.

- Urge your child to be active. If his asthma is well controlled, he should be able to take part in most activities. Exercise is necessary for your child's health and self-esteem.

ASTHMA IN SENIORS

Some people don't get asthma until their senior years. Seniors who have poorly controlled asthma may think of themselves in poor health, and have a harder time with daily activities. Even though lung function does go down after the age of 40, there are things seniors can do to improve their asthma symptoms.

- **Lower exposure to indoor triggers** such as older furnishings, high indoor humidity, mold, older mattresses, cockroaches, and pets with fur.

- **Report asthma symptoms to your doctor.** Older people may feel that the symptoms they're having are part of normal aging, so they may not report their symptoms. Many seniors don't take the proper medications to control their allergy and asthma signs. They may rely too heavily on quick-relief medications.

- **Get a total check-up.** Seniors may have other health problems that affect their asthma. Some physical problems (eyesight, arthritis and poor hearing) may make it hard to follow instructions or use medical devices. Talk to your doctor and respiratory therapist about these problems.

- **Talk to your doctor about preventing lung infections by getting flu and pneumonia shots.**

- **Write down instructions for taking medications if you have problems remembering.**

- **Eat well.** A healthy well-balanced diet can stop some asthma symptoms and help you stay fit.

- **Stay as active as you can.** Staying physically active is good for mind, body and spirit. It's no different with asthma. Keep moving and you'll be better able to take care of the condition.

- **Learn about your medicine.** Ask your physician or pharmacist if any of your prescription medicine could interfere with your asthma control.

ASTHMA IN PREGNANCY
BABY ON THE WAY, ASTHMA NOT OKAY!

The bad news about being pregnant while having asthma is that symptoms may become worse for about a third of pregnant women. Not keeping your asthma in check can be harmful to both your health and that of your baby.

HOW TO BETTER MANAGE YOUR ASTHMA WHILE PREGNANT

- Tell your doctor or nurse that you have asthma.
- Plan regular visits to your doctor for your asthma and the care of your unborn baby.
- Talk to your doctor about the medicines you take for your asthma.
- Keep taking your asthma medication. Most medicines for asthma are safe to take when you're pregnant as long as you follow your doctor's advice.
REMEMBER: If your asthma is not under control, your lungs aren't getting enough oxygen to your baby, which is a far greater risk than taking the asthma medications.
- Try not to take over-the-counter medications while pregnant. These asthma/allergy and cold medications contain drugs that break up or lower extra mucus and may be harmful to your baby.
- Stay away from certain antibiotics, such as tetracycline.
- Don't receive live virus vaccines, only killed virus vaccines.
- Don't start allergy shots during pregnancy. If you were getting them before your pregnancy, you may be able to keep taking them under the supervision of your doctor.
- Be extra careful to stay away from things that may trigger an asthma episode.

DON'T WORRY

- Wheezing during labor and delivery is rare.
- Most asthma medicines will not harm your baby.
- If you breastfeed, asthma medicines will not cause problems for your baby.

ACKNOWLEDGEMENTS

This booklet contains information adapted from:

- The Global Initiative for Management of Asthma. A Practical Guide for Public Health Officials and Health Care Professionals. National Institutes of Health and World Organizations, 1998.

- National Heart Lung and Blood Institute (NHLBI) of the National Institutes of Health (NIH). Expert Panel Report 3: Guidelines for the Diagnosis and Management of Asthma- Full Report 2007.

- Peak Performance USA, A Program for Managing Asthma in the School. American Association for Respiratory Care, Dallas, TX.

Information

The information contained in this booklet is for general reference purposes only. This booklet is not intended as a substitute for professional medical care. Only your doctor can diagnose and treat a medical problem.

Nurtur's policy prohibits staff members from actively advertising, marketing, or promoting specific products or services to our members or their physicians when discussing the member's health condition.

Medical Review
The content of this booklet was reviewed by Woody Kageler, MD, FACP, FCCP.

Special Thanks
Special thanks to Dr. Woody Kageler, Kaneshia Agnew, Dana Oliver and Jennifer Allen for their contributions to the revision of this guide.

FURTHER HELP

For information and answers to questions you have about asthma, contact any of these groups:

Nurtur
1-800-293-0056
nurturhealth.com

American Lung Association
1-800-LUNG-USA (1-800-586-4872)
lungusa.org/

National Heart, Lung, and Blood Institute
NHLBI Information Center
P.O. Box 30105
Bethesda, MD 20824-0105
www.nhlbi.nih.gov/health/index.htm

American Academy of Allergy, Asthma and Immunology
aaaai.org

Asthma and Allergy Foundation of America
aafa.org

Allergy and Asthma Network, Mothers of Asthmatics Inc.
aanma.org

American College of Allergy, Asthma and Immunology
acaai.org

CALL US WHEN:

- ◉ You have an increase in symptoms

- ◉ You receive new medications

- ◉ You have questions as to your breathing

- ◉ Your phone number, address or Primary Care Physician changes

- ◉ You have asthma and your peak flow drops into your yellow zone or red zone

CALL THE NUMBER LISTED BELOW

COMPLETE THE CARD BELOW

The card printed below is for you to supply medical staff with key information about yourself and medicines you take.

Once you fill out the card, simply cut it out along the dashed line, fold it and place it in your wallet or purse. Carry it with you at all times.

My name: _____

My doctor's name: _____

    Phone #: _____

Emergency Contact's name: _____

    Phone #: _____

I have these health conditions: Asthma

Allergies: _____

FILL OUT ALL YOUR INFORMATION!

I take these medicines:

MEDICINE NAME	HOW MUCH?	HOW OFTEN?